Healing While Grieving

A Spiritual Therapeutic Approach Through the Journey of Grief

I0435382

By: Rev. Angel Onley-Livingston, MA, LPC, NCC

Thanks and Acknowledgements

To my husband Kevin, I thank you for allowing me to continue to type when you were trying to sleep. I thank those who have fought the good fight of faith in life who have now transitioned to give me the right to process their significance in my life. To my mother, Martha, thanks for listening to me complain about the struggle of writing this book. I thank Aunt Sue, Aunt Edith, Aunt Gwen, Aunt Leola, Uncle Charles, Aunt Sylvia, Aunt Rosa Lee, Cousin Linda, Mama Cat, Mama Joann, Cousin Reginald, Aunt Noonie, Uncle Box, Rev. H.H. Singleton II, Cheeta, Gwen Dean, Cousin Marionette, and all of the other elders in my life who have gone on to be in the great cloud of witnesses. Oh, how I live my life, to see you again and to celebrate!

Table of Contents

Foreword

Rev. Angel Onley-Livingston is a breath of fresh air. Healing While Grieving is a breath of fresh air! At some point in life everyone experiences death. The grief you experience after a death is rarely talked about. People assume that after you get through the funeral everything goes back to 'normal' or that you are 'ok'. The truth is that after the funeral is when the real grief sets in. During those first few hours or days, you are simply numb with disbelief. Processing your thoughts and feelings takes a back seat to simply making it through the decisions and legions of people paying their respects.

Along with the death of loved-ones comes the grieving process and the pinned up emotions of anger, guilt, loss, pain and numbness. Healing While Grieving walks you through that process while allowing you to connect to your emotions, to your pain, to your faith and to God. Doing so allows you to reconnect with you, the one grieving. The therapeutic exercises are simple yet profound in their effect. The act of writing, doing, connecting, expressing and accepting leads one back to a place of homeostasis. Healing While Grieving takes you from the depths of pain and despair to a place of hope and healing.

I only wish I had this book to read years ago. When my stepfather died in a tragic accident, I struggled in silence for many months. Understanding the grieving process and working through exercises would have been vastly beneficial had I had this book. Pushing my grief down left me feeling empty, sad, lonely and depressed. I fought my way out of darkness. However since that time 10 years ago I learned that internalizing grief only prolongs its duration. *Healing While Grieving* is the beacon in the night that you need while grieving that will guide you back into the light of day.

Regardless of any religious beliefs or affiliations, this book will connect with you. Through the therapeutic exercises you experience God in truth, in life and in love. This is a spiritual work that will guide you through your dark days and nights as you navigate down the road paved by the death of your loved-one. *Healing While Grieving* is one of those books that you can turn to again and again to help you regain your joy. Death is a part of the circle of life. You need this book to help you navigate through your circle of life.

Kimberly Dixon, M.Ed, CPC, CCRC
Joyful Living with Kimberly Dixon, LLC

Preface

I am writing this book as a source of narrative therapeutic healing for myself, though I pray this will be a source of healing for you. It was around the year of 1997 that I began losing loved ones, or was at a point in my life when I began to feel the sting of the absence of loved ones around me. 2009-2015 have been some of the hardest years of my life. I lost pillars of my family, mentors that I looked up to in the community to the death and dying process, which led me to the grief and healing process. The process was healing while grieving for me because I was birthing children as elders were transitioning out of my family. The major transition that happened for me was what happens to every family after a death, I grew closer to some and some relationships just simply fell apart. This small book of personal meditations and coping skills mixed with my clinical background is what allowed me to heal while grieving. I am not done yet through this grieving process, so I wrote some of these pages as the waves of grief continued to flow. I pray that this book will allow you to heal while grieving as well.

Introduction

This book is meant to be a vessel to incorporate many forms of therapeutic skills, cultural, religious, and spiritual forms into your daily devotional or meditation time when dealing with the loss of a loved one. Grief can bring on and out so many thoughts, emotions, feelings, and memories that will sometimes flood you. At times you might not even be able to form the words to express how you feel. However, it is important that you take time to reflect, breathe, be silent, scream, and cry. Yes, these devotionals will help you do all of these things.

Grieving happens in many different forms and for different time periods for each individual. Sometimes while reading through this devotional and doing the healing exercises, you may feel the need to reach out to talk to a loved one, pastor, priest, spiritual guide, counselor, or psychiatrist. This is normal. Everyone gets to a point in their life while processing grief where they feel like they may have lost their way, their faith, and might even be angry at God, the universe, or family or loved ones. This book will give you some easy exercises, biblical references, and spiritual insight to help you navigate this part of life. So I pray you enjoy this journey of healing while grieving.

Grieving as a Journey of Healing

Grieving is like a journey. Journeys never really end. We go through phases of the journey as we reflect, remember, and search for God in the midst of the journey. It is while we are looking for God that we become the one that is actually found. We are 'found' in God's presence seeking God's grace, mercy, love, healing, and transformation. There are moments where it is very dark, gloomy, and lonely rather by choice or force. There will be moments where you will want to celebrate the loved one and dance and laugh, and moments when it feels like you just want to give up.

The important thing to remember is to listen to your body and to your soul. Give it what it needs. If you feel the urge to be by water and just be silent, or to immerse yourself in it for a cleansing, renewed feeling, DO IT. Do what the body needs. If your soul needs rest or a refreshing consider prayer, meditation, sitting in silence, and sometimes being around others of like-mindedness.

Experience the Moment:

I want to help you at this moment find your safe place. A safe place is a physical or mental place that you can go to heal. In this moment sit still, listen, and observe what your body feels and needs. Begin to take a deep breath in through your nose and blow out through your mouth slowly. Take in all of the sounds or the lack thereof. Adjust yourself to what you need. Allow your body to move and do what it needs to do. If you need to speak words to give your emotion a voice, do that. If you feel the need to run, scream, yell, jump, or pound on something, DO IT! Anxiety sets in when we won't allow our emotions the opportunity to flow naturally.

Find a street or beach and run. Find a pillow to scream or yell in, or, a place where you can scream and yell without interference or alarming others. When anxiety or emotions that we can't describe are lodged in our bodies, sometimes we need to dance, jump, move, and sway our body to our emotions free. Remember there is no right or wrong way to do this. If you need to pound on something, consider getting some modeling clay and making something. The pulling and tugging at the clay without any intention of making anything is a therapeutic expressive art skill in itself. The point is to get still enough to listen to what your body and soul needs at that moment and do it.

Joy Comes in the Morning
"… Weeping may last through the night, but joy comes with the morning."
Psalm 30:5 New Living Translation

Have you ever noticed that after a bad storm, a huge break up, or the loss of something or someone, that as the sun rises either we are accepting of the fullness of that sunrise, or we are fearful of what it may bring. The truth is joy is there regardless if we accept it or not. Joy overtakes you the moment you accept it. Joy is better than happiness or gladness. Joy goes beyond the skin to the soul deep. Joy is the knowing that the Great Divine God decided to create us for a particular purpose on earth. God wants to see you rejoice, not down and depressed, that is why God has given you joy, unspeakable joy. Joy is that feeling, thought, or emotion, when you use utterances and sounds to express the level of the depth of your soul.

The Healing Exercise:

I want you to find your joy. Joy was given to you by the great God, our creator. We have to acknowledge that there is a Great One, out there, one greater than anyone or anything else. We then have to acknowledge, welcome, and accept, the light that shines from the Great One, God, Creator, Omnipresent, and Omniscient One. That light is the essence of God, the Holy Spirit, who gives us Joy. Now, take it in. Breathe it in deep. Feel God, the Lord, the Light, the Holy Spirit, the ever moving, ever presence, never leaving comforting spirit. Now, Exhale and let everything out that does not shine light like the Joy of God!

Silent Prayers

Silent prayers are sometimes the hardest prayers. Silent prayers are the small bits of breath that we can sometimes get out in the moments of depression and grief when we have nothing left. It's that moment when our thoughts, feelings, emotions, escape and abandon us. Silent prayer can also be the greatest prayer, because it is received by God in such a way that we are yielding ourselves to listen. It's the prayer that sometimes touches the most hearts in a crowd. It's the prayer that a mother whispers in her heart while burying one of her children. Silent prayers are the prayers we say when we are just not sure of how much more we can take. The importance though, behind the silence in those prayers, is the very essence that we have the faith to yield to God in a posture of prayer. It is in silent prayers that we approach God's throne boldly with the expectation that we are praying to a God who already knows.

Gathering Your Faith Exercise:

When we lose someone very dear to us, it cuts us to our very core to reflect on our own personal lives. It's in the moments when we just want to roll and curl up in a fetal position, sob, and scream, or ask God, "Why did you take them from me." These are the very moments we need to run to the things that ground us in our faith. Right now I want you to do something spiritual. Go and find the things that ground you in your faith. If you don't have a faith background or a personal relationship with God, this is the moment that will help you on your spiritual journey.

I want you to make a collage of things using whatever materials you have. Getting out in public or in fresh air is always good while grieving. Take a walk, gather some things from nature that seem solid or that speak to your inner self. Another option is to make a list of items you need and go to the local craft store.

However you decide to do this, make something, create something to fill those empty places that are now void due to the loss of a loved one. You see you have to get moving, get up and do something.

Do not let your silent prayers turn into more silent pain, by choosing to fill those empty spaces with things that will make you more empty: excessive drinking, drugs, recreational sexual pleasures, excessive eating, and oh so much more. You know your temptations. Write them down as your Poison Choices List of things to avoid indulging in during this time.

3:00 AM Can't Sleep

In the still of the early morning while most people are asleep can be the hardest time for someone who is grieving. These are the moments when things are silent. The place where a warm body once laid is now just cold sheets. The smell of their perfume or cologne is still there, but there is no physical body. This is the moment that you question what will today bring and how will I get through it. The number 3 in many religions, sacred practices represents authority, balance, structure, order, creativity, and an opening in the multidimensional aspects of time. God exists outside of time, and so does our soul. Therefore, I believe that this is the window of time that allows us to bring what we need to reorder, change, and set forth for our day what should be done in this hour.

It's in this hour that you should speak things into existence. This is the moment that your soul, which is housed in your body is more awakened and prevalent than your body. This is the hour to meditate, retrain your thought patterns, sit in silence, pray, and discern.

The Healing Exercise:

Though this process may be hard, it creates discipline. It gives structure, order, and direction. Maybe you can't do 3 AM, pick a time during your day to do something to honor God and do something Holy. God resides on the inside of you! God created you, so you are a living representation of God as a little god in the earth. This is the hour to begin to declare, "Thy Kingdom Come on Earth as it is in Heaven," as Jesus prayed. This is the hour where your imagination and creative self will take over to help you formulate goals, decisions, and directions to replace the empty places and spaces that were once filled by the one whom you grieve.

The Five Stages of Grief

"There are no goodbyes for us. Wherever you are, You will always be in our hearts."
-Mahatma Gandhi

Our heart is where we hold our biggest desires and our biggest hurts. It's in our hearts that we carry the memories of our departed loved ones. Denial, Anger, Bargaining, Depression, Acceptance, these are the basic 5 stages of grief. Sometimes we feel these stages all at once, then again we might feel one more strongly than others. Denial hits just when it becomes too hard to imagine our loved one gone. It's when we begin to think of all the things we haven't finished with them, or all the things they didn't get a chance to teach us. Anger boils up when we begin to question ourselves, others, God, and even the universe as to why they had to leave so suddenly.

Bargaining, sounds like, "God, I just need one more visit with them please, then I will do whatever you want me to do. " God, take me instead." "God, I can think of several others you can take, but not her." These are the words I have heard all too many times from many different families while sitting during the transitioning moments. Depression is that lonely dark place that we want to just crawl up in our beds and just die along with them. We forget how to move on, that we have a reason to live, and we want the world to stop, or we stop living. Last, but not least acceptance is when we can celebrate the life of our loved one. Acceptance brings joy, peace, comfort, and the ability to embrace reality.

Confrontation Exercise:

Now, it's time to survey yourself. See where you currently are in the grieving process. Identify which stage you are in and accept it. Face it. Surrender to its process. Allow the emotions that you have been burying, stuffing down on the inside, choking down, to come up and OUT! It's time to heal, beloved.

You cannot heal what you are not willing to face. It's time to look yourself in the mirror and have a conversation with self. Create sticky notes with daily affirmations and put them up around your dwelling place so that you can see the truth even when you don't want to.

Why Does it Hurt So Bad?

I wanted to cry, I simply wanted to. The tears never came, it hurt too bad to cry. I wanted to say words of encouragement, but no words would come that I could say to convince myself, forget encouraging the family. They wanted me to pray, and all I could ask God was, "Why does it hurt so bad?" These are words from a journal entry I did inside my head, but never put ink to paper to write it down. I can remember standing in my aunt's hospital room wanting to scream, yell, tell God that I couldn't take anymore. Instead I prayed, as they asked, "God, thy will be done." As I walked out of the hospital room I felt like I was going to simply pass out. I can remember walking ahead of others and then slowly gripping the rails along the wall for strength. Then, it happened. I held on to the railing for dear life and allowed all the sounds and emotion to come up and out and all at once. Someone grabbed me, and whispered, "You have to be strong for your mom." I don't recall who it was, but for the first time I didn't feel like the preacher, the prayer warrior, the strong one, I'd had enough of death. I wanted to finally say how I felt, how my body felt, how my heart was broken. I wanted to scream from the hospital halls to death, "Go away from me!"

This time I needed to just be plain old Angel. The soul having a human experience. I needed to fall into someone else's arms and just cry until I couldn't cry another tear. That is what I did until I got tired of the pain. Until I decided to let healing take place. I made a mental and heartfelt decision to embrace what was left of our family and do my part to have meaningful relationships. I chose to live and give the hurt a place to be poured out through putting my hands into some modeling clay and creating something that represented the good, the bad, the ugly, and the beauty of the circle of life.

Pour Out Your Heart Exercise:

Today I want you to give yourself permission to find out why it hurts so bad, what hurts, and how to process the hurt. Search, dig for the beauty in the ashes and pour yourself into the beauty of what can now be. Get closer to loved ones of friends who are still around and talk about your pain and how others have learned to cope and process their grief. Healing happens when we talk, dialog, discuss how things affect us. It's time now beloved to let your soul see the richness of having a human experience of healing while grieving.

My Talk with Death

"...Oh death where is your sting..."

1 Corinthians 15:55 NLT

Where is your sting? Where is your sting? Well death let me tell you where your sting is, not in them, you have no power over them, but I feel your sting. I feel the pain, the hurt, the emptiness, the barrenness. I feel the loss of not hearing their voices, or seeing them at family gatherings. I no longer have their hands or hair to touch. I feel the silence where their voices once filled my life in the morning or afternoons.

I feel your STING! You have taken them from me. Though you cannot hold them or keep them, though God gave you permission to come for them, I now realize that the sting and the hold is now on me. After losing to you aunt Edith, cousin Linda, Aunt Rosa Lee, Aunt Gwen, Aunt Leola, Mama Cat, cousin Reginald, Uncle Jimmy, Aunt Noonie, Uncle Box, Uncle Cheeta, and now you take my Aunt Joann?

Really? You just wipe out the whole foundation, anchor, and wisdom seats of our family? I had so many questions. I WASN'T FINISHED with loving them yet. Then, death spoke back. As I was outside sweating, pushing a lawn mower in 85 degree weather, fussing at death in my head and heart, I got tired and no matter how hard I worked it's like the yard still wasn't done. I ran from the yard and took my shoes off on the porch. As I ran into the house for something to drink and sat on my favorite couch, out of habit, I heard death speak. Death spoke, "See, that's why I came. Just like you were tired though you knew you had a job to do (while mowing the lawn), that is how they were living. They were struggling to finish the race. They were tired, though they kept loving, running, and waiting patiently for others to love one another and truly care for one another."

"Their bodies gave out on them, not the other way around. I had to come. Yes your yard is still not done, just as they fought, but still left some work undone, though that work was not theirs to do." Then I sat quiet. I felt convicted and now ashamed that I was really asking the question to death. I continued as I asked, "What about me now?" "What does this mean for me? Why does my life have to change? What is the point of all of this pain?"

Then, death responded, "So that they could feel no more pain. So that their tears would no longer flow out of sorrow. Now, their hearts no longer break and now they can be free from the burdens of this world." Now I know the sting is there to remind me of how quickly death can come. The sting reminds me daily to not just exist, but to LIVE. What I have learned from my talk with death is that this is one thing in life that is inevitable, but we get to choose how we respond and use it's sting.

"Fight Back!"

Death can sometimes block us from the realization that we have to fight back to get back! Fight to breathe, fight to live, fight to move on, and fight to recreate a life without the one we love. We are to fight back with a new zest for life and to use the extra love that we now have to fill up someone else's life.

See, it is hard to see the situation from the victory perspective. We must not only see what we have lost and what has been spilled out, but the fact that now we have more room to fill it up with love for someone and something else. When we love hard, it takes so much out of us; time, energy, gifts, phone calls, visits, letters, emails, text messages, video calls, and much more. Now, if we could total up all of that time and look at our wish lists, vision boards, bucket lists, and fight back by using all of this love to get back out there and fight for the kind of life we must go on and Live!

The Healing Exercise:

Today, I want you to create that list, vision board, wish list, living list, and fight back. Show yourself that there is still much more to live for. When you are sad, pick something from the list and begin researching, planning, and live it up! It's not your time to go yet! You have to Fight! Get back up! Get out of bed, and LIVE!

The Five Senses

In my counseling practice, I often use what I call the Five Senses Technique when dealing with people who have experienced, witness, or felt like their life was threatened by a traumatic experience. Trauma gets lodged in our bodies as well as our thoughts. We feel, see, taste, smell, and hear traumatic experiences. In my therapeutic approach I ask five very specific things. I ask, "What did it sound like, taste like, feel like to the touch, look like, smell like?" This may sound weird, but when we go through something traumatic, we process it through our five senses. The good news is we can also use these same senses to heal and to create a safe space and to separate the false signals, feelings, and emotions, from the real ones.

The Healing Therapeutic Exercise:

When you got that phone call, stood by that bedside, speeded down the highway to be with your loved one, every one of your five senses experienced it. Today, List the five senses across the top of your paper. Divide into columns. Now I want you to write down everything that comes to mind during the experience when you lost your loved one in each respective column. Sit with it, allow your body to acknowledge that you know it. Say a prayer, light a candle, release the pain from those places with verbally stating: "I release the pain of _____ or I release the pain from my_____." Now, take note of where you feel that pain going to in your body. Listen to your body- it knows what it needs to heal. Take a walk, get a massage, talk with your health care professional, counselor, Angel Light Healer, Reiki Master, and release the pain. Then, repeat the phrase above for each of the 5 senses. For smell release and replace that smell with a smell of an aroma therapeutic oil. Please note while doing these exercises if it becomes more than you can handle alone seek professional help for healing.

Pictures on the Walls

There is that moment, when you have come to acceptance of the death of your loved one. You are back in your daily routine and you can get through most of your day realizing that you must live on. Then, you run in the door to grab something and you see their picture on the wall. Pictures are very important during the grieving process, it helps us face the fear of us forgetting what our loved ones looked like, the way they wore their hair, or their style of clothing. Pictures of our loved ones also bring us to a pause of remembrance of how short our lives really are. It causes us to examine our pictures, how we have aged, and we even look for resemblances of them in our features, style of clothing, and in our essence of being.

The Healing Therapeutic Exercise:

Today I want you to take a picture of your loved one and spend some time with it. Remember their voice, their smell, their face. Remember how it felt to be embraced by them. Then, I want you to create a poem, letter, scrapbook page, something to give homage to them. This however is more for them than you. I want you to tell them how you are doing and progressing and healing through this thing called grief, so that they can journey on. You must let them know that you are okay and that you are strong enough to go on living to create your own pictures on your walls.

Dreams, Visions, and Sounds

When we have lost a loved one, we often dream about them as though they are still alive. Sometimes we follow behind a car on the road that we just know is theirs. Often times we hear sounds of their laughter or their voice and we begin to search to find them. Often while I am grieving I can still hear my loved one's voices. I could hear their laughter and sometimes when the house was quiet I swore I could hear them coming down the hallway.

Then, there were times when I would dream about those who have departed. Some dreams would be dreams of remembrance of times we were together, and some it seemed as if they were leading me somewhere or trying to answer a question I had asked God.

One thing I believe, is that the spirit world is greater than we could ever comprehend. Who is to say, that it isn't their footsteps I hear when I need to be comforted by them? Or that morning when I was sure I saw my cousin's car turning into the school building where she worked on a morning that I felt low and down, I followed it, when she didn't get out it was then, and only then, that I remembered she was gone.

Believe in the Vastness of the Spirit Realm Exercise:

We all have been taught through some form of religion or forms of religions how and what happens to our ancestors or our loved ones after they have ceased to live in their earthly bodies. Today, I challenge you to come up with your theological expression of what it is you actually believe, so that acceptance of the death can come more easily. Sometimes we are stuck in anger or denial, simply because we don't have the information to put words to our feelings, or because we have no foundation of what faith really means to us. Not what we have been taught, but our own personal experience with God. Today, I want you to spend some time with God alone. Not with a priest, pastor, nun, guru, mom, dad, grandma, or wisdom bearer. I want you to seek God for yourself and get the answers you need to decide what you really think or know you believe. Give yourself time to experience nature, new people, and new places. God is everywhere, if you would only give yourself the opportunity to go through the process of knocking, seeking, and finding.

Keeping Thyself in Perfect Peace

When trying to heal while grieving there are sometimes moments when relationships with friends, family, spouses, and children can be strained, non-existent, and even overbearing. These are the moments when families get closer, or they just simply fall apart. It's during the time of grieving that we begin to have the freedom to redefine what family, love, faith, and devotion really mean to us. We get to shed expectations and the way mama, daddy, grandma, grandpa, sister, cousin, and so on, did things. We get the opportunity to rewrite the next phase of our life. Death sometimes reveals things that were said in private, to some and not others, and things that were unspoken. This may happen during the reading of a will, cleaning out books and finding a journal, or when the matriarch of the family has passed and no one steps up to take the lead, or the one who takes the lead isn't necessarily the one that others would have chosen.

These are tender moments. Moments when all stages of grief are evident in different stages in different people. It's sometimes like walking on eggshells and for some they just simply stay away from engaging in any part of the process of saying Goodbye. These moments can be treasured or they can add fuel to a fire that was lit years ago. It's important that you decide what is important to you and consider the wishes of the loved one who has departed.

After the fire has been lit, words begin to fly, or relatives leave because their names weren't mentioned. This is the time to seek God's guidance in how to keep your personal peace and remain true to who you know you are. This is the time that you reach out and love without any expectations. Something we don't always see until after the matriarch of the family is gone, is how much that matriarch understood the love languages of everyone. They knew how to give love to others in the way others needed love. Sometimes the best way to help a situation is to just be present, speak, show, give, and become love.

The Healing Process for Putting Out Fires:

Remember the only one you can control is yourself. You cannot change the thoughts of others, if they don't understand and accept that there are other opinions besides their own. Ask yourself, "Did I invite myself into this fire, or was I thrown into it?" "Do I have a right to say something about this situation?" "Who do they (those closely affected by the death) need me to be at this very moment?" See these questions can save you a lot of headache and heartache. Sometimes the best way to put out a fire, is to check and see if you have the gasoline, or the water, and choose and act, accordingly.

The Silence of Death This Way Comes

It's mornings like these, where I go to pick up the phone and dial a number that out of habit I expect to hear a voice return of, "Hello." Though as I walk across the room to dial the number the sickening feeling and silence of death reminds me that they are no longer able to answer the phone. The silence that comes in missing your loved one's voice sometimes can feel as if someone knocks the wind right out of your chest. You still reach for the phone, drive by their house, job, or where you normally met for lunch or after work, only to remember they are not there.

Sometimes this is the thing that grips you and feels like it suffocates you. This is the moment when you try not to erase the voices of your loved ones on the answering machine and you play it over and over again. I know I did. Wondering if what I was doing when I decided to not answer my phone, or couldn't answer my phone, if it was really that important. Had I known that was the last time I would hear them speak, breathe, laugh, cry. Now...I will be more careful to reverence the voice of God in others.

When it Hurts Like Hell Meditation:

Simply allow yourself time to grieve. That's it. Sit, have a cry, drink some tea or coffee. Go for a walk, lay back in bed, take the extra 5 minutes before beginning work. Just do it. In order to heal you must experience the silence. You must train your mind, body, and spirit, to get use to the absence of their body, but not their soul. Reverence God's imprint, God's image in them...their soul. Ask them for forgiveness, guidance, love, light, then forgive yourself, love on yourself, and push through the day.

The Wave of Grief

Denial, anger, guilt, depression, acceptance, over and over again. Maybe not necessarily in that order, but it just hits you when it decides to. Maybe you smelled a perfume, saw a car passing, heard a song. Mine comes when I decide to go to a Christian worship gathering or event and they would play a song called, "This Place," by Tamela Mann. I would become overly emotional. I would have to run out of the service, or sob for the whole hour, or simply yell, and scream, on the inside as I would fight back tears. Sometimes I would just go numb all together. I didn't know which one would happen or when it would happen, I just knew it was coming.

I could be simply having a conversation with someone and the person that had transitioned, their name would slip out of my mouth during our dialogue, and I would have to take a deep breath, look away, shake it off. The flood of emotions were and are sometimes just too much to bear. One of the coping mechanisms that I use is to revert to something that was funny or inspirational to me about them. I would tell the story and laugh until I cried and that is when I knew that the sting of death's wave of grief was just a little less hurtful. Try it sometimes. Remember the good write them a letter as if they were alive to read it. Read it aloud to your children who never got a chance to know them. These coping tools are like a balm on an open sore. It gives relief to the place that needs to heal.

A Simple Prayer:

God, in your mercy, hear my prayer. I need you to guide me through this wave. Help me to be slow to anger and to grow stronger in the acceptance of the death of my loved ones. Please of God help me in the moments when I don't know what to do or say. God I pray that I can trust you in the midst of what might even be depression and give me the strength to ask for help when I can no longer manage or cope. Lord, here is my prayer. Amen.

Selah

I hope that this devotional has helped you begin the process of healing while grieving. That you will lift up your head, give praise to God, and weigh in the balances of life. This devotional was instrumental in helping me process many lives that I grieve and celebrate. Grief took me on a spiritual journey that allowed my soul and mind to open up far beyond what I had been taught by church and the Christian faith community. Grieving allowed me to explore forms of meditation, acupuncture, expressive arts, playing again, and to ask questions that I was once scared to even ask God. Grieving takes us to many different places in our mind, it gets trapped in our body, and we must use our soul to guide us through the corridors of healing through healthy grieving.

Today, I pray that you use this book as an instrument, a guide, a light on your path of healing. Remember grieving is different for everyone. Do not hesitate to seek help from professionals, spiritual leaders, family matriarchs, and deep inside your soul. Surround yourself with others who have walked this journey of grieving, who are healthy and well, and ask questions and even seek their help as an accountability partner through this process.

Godspeed on your journey to healing while grieving.

The Author

Author Rev. Angel Onley--Livingston, MA, LPC, NCC

Professional Services Provided

Individual Counseling, Family Counseling, Couples Counseling, Spiritual Life Coaching, Angel Light Healing (Energy Work), Focusing and Grounding Techniques, Skills to decrease Anger, Anxiety, and Depression, Spiritual Retreats, Brief Solution Focused Therapy Techniques, Life Transitions such as Grief, Loss, College, Marriage and Divorce. Focusing and Grounding Techniques, Skills to overcome blockages due to Anger, Anxiety, and Depression, Ancestor Spirit Circle, Prayer Vigils/Ceremony, Marriage Ceremony Officiant in South Carolina.

Personal Therapeutic Theory

Rev. Angel Onley-Livingston meets her clients where they are in their life and helps them to develop a plan and put it into action to live the kind of life they want. She is here to listen. She is here to educate. She is here as a reflective mirror to give you back your own words, reflections on your life stories, accompanied with educational information for you to be able to reflect, think, make decisions, and live your best life! With over 9 years of Professional Counseling and over 11 years of Spiritual Counseling experience, she allows mental health counseling to meet the spiritual world in her therapeutic skills.

Using skills from expressive art forms, talk therapy through Cognitive Behavioral Therapy, and spiritual practices, she treats the whole person. The niche she has found after 11 years in this field is in working with adolescents, adults and couples. Angel currently practices in a partnership at Coastal Carolina OBGYN LLC as their National Board Certified Counselor, and runs her private practice House of Abba LLC. where she treats children, teens, and families in their homes.

Educational Background:

Angel is a National Board Certified Counselor and A Licensed Professional Counselor in the State of South Carolina. Angel's education background is comprehensive with a B.A. in Interdisciplinary Studies with an emphasis in Early Childhood Education and Psychology from Coastal Carolina University. She has also completed a Masters in Professional Counseling with a minor in Mental Health from Webster University. She furthered her Spiritual Discernment by completing her first year of requirements of a two year Seminary Degree in Masters of Arts in Religion Program of Lutheran Theological Southern Seminary. Reverend Onley--Livingston was licensed to preach the gospel in 2007 at Friendship Missionary Baptist Church of Conway, SC. She was then ordained to the gospel ministry in November of 2011 at Palmetto Missionary Baptist Church of Conway, SC.

Rev. Onley--Livingston was trained in Applied Behavioral Therapy through Horry County Schools where she served as a therapist and Lead Therapist during the implementation years of the Learning Lab, which used a Cognitive Behavioral Approach to Behavioral Therapy, at Myrtle Beach Primary School and Carolina Forest Middle School. Reverend Angel Onley-Livingston has received Trauma-Focused Cognitive Behavioral Therapy training through an in-service training provided by MUSC at Waccamaw Mental Health.

Angel provided mental health counseling services through the Child and Adolescents Department of Waccamaw Mental Health Center by providing services in Horry County Schools through the Safe Schools Healthy Students Grant.

Rev. Onley-Livingston has experience from her previous employment in alcohol and substance abuse counseling in clinical service settings where she received alcohol and substance abuse training and supervision. Angel provided individual and group services at Shoreline Behavioral Health Services through the Safe Schools Health Students Grant where she provided services for clients in all of the Middle and High School settings of Horry County Schools and in their homes and alternative residential placements. Rev. Onley-Livingston also has experience with the treatment of alcohol and drug patients in the process of assessment, treatment, and consultation of clients who were being treated with Methadone at The Center of Hope in Myrtle Beach, SC.

Angel completed the PEAT Program in July of 2015 where she obtained a Certificate in Play & Expressive Arts Therapies, A fertile ground for emerging growth. She obtained 30 hour Training Program- CEU's. This program focuses on the integration of play & expressive arts practices in therapies for adolescents, adults, and couples. It is principally an experiential program, accompanied by some conversations about brain-wise practices in therapy. Trainings included learning The Body as a Source of Wisdom & Expressive Arts: Weaving a Home Grown Self, Journeying through Wounds, Personal Mythologies, Silenced Stories, Big Dreams, & Alchemical Transformations, Symbolic & Imaginable Worlds: Liberation Arts: Our Personal, Interpersonal, & Transpersonal Practices. In October 2015, she completed the Prepare & Enrich training to be a facilitator to help couples live a whole and healthy marriage. Angel's proposal to the South Carolina Counseling Association to present at the 2016 Conference was accepted and she will present on 'Grieving in Many Forms."

Links that will help with the healing process:

http://www.simplyaroma.com/index.aspx

http://www.houseofabba.com/

https://www.facebook.com/ReverendAOL/

https://www.facebook.com/HouseOfAbbaCounselingCenterLlc/

www.ingramcontent.com/pod-product-compliance
Lightning Source LLC
Chambersburg PA
CBHW071321280526
45788CB00004B/1972